Thank You For Reading This Book.

Please Visit:
www.RandallKowalenko.com
To sign up for my Internet Marketing
E-Zine Today!

I0463151

60 FREE
And Low Cost Ways To
Market
Your
Online
Newsletter
or E-Zine

By: Randall Kowalenko

LEGAL NOTICE

Table of Contents

Dedication

This book is dedicated to you & your online newsletter marketing success!

For God so loved the world that he gave his one and only Son, that whoever believes in him shall not perish but have eternal life. John 3:16 (NIV)

Please visit **www.NeedHim.org** for more information about salvation today!

Forward

Paper newsletters are quickly being replaced with online newsletters - that's a fact that's here to stay.

But unfortunately, many people are not maximizing their online newsletter's reach & influence because they are not marketing it as well as they could be.

If building a mailing list is not one of your top priorities in your line of business IT SHOULD BE...

Marketing to your mailing list is truly a numbers game, where two important variables are the number of subscribers you have, and the conversion rate (the percentage of subscribers who purchase your product or service).

The name of the game is to gernerate a quality targeted list for your desired market, and to build it as big and quickly as possible.

That's where the confusion often comes

in. While many people setup a quality newsletter program (or outsource it) they neglect to market it. Online newsletters are great, but many people need direction on how to effectively market them, yet in free or low cost ways.

That's Where This Book Comes In.

The purpose of this book is to uncover practical ways to market your online newsletter without breaking your bank account in the process.

It is no more effort to send your newsletter to 1,000 people than it is to send it to only 100. If you are already making the effort to publish an online newsletter why not strive for this tool to be your own personal ten thousand pound gorilla lead generation system that works for you relentlessly to bring in a flow of business from pre-qualified leads who frequently approach you instead of the other way around?

Keep this book close, and employ these techniques to your own online newsletter program to produce marketing results that can have a significant effect on your bottom line for years to come.

Looking forward to your success!

Randall Kowalenko

Important Notice

This book is practical and useful for both online newsletters & ezines.

In an effort to keep the writing simple, clear and with minimal fluff I only reference 'newsletters' in the writing of this text instead of 'newsletters & ezines', although the principals apply equally to both.

I am not saying newsletters are better or worse than ezines, but since more people are familiar with the term 'newsletters' that is the language I have decided to use in this text. Enjoy!

Idea #1

Offer A Contest With Recognition For The Most Referrals

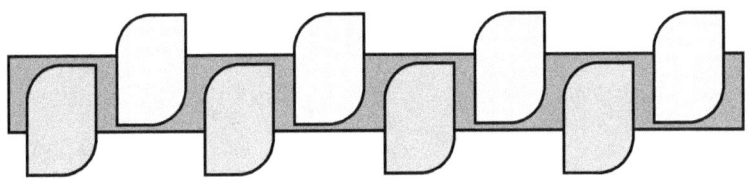

People aren't getting enough recognition but they love it!

Offer a contest where in every issue of your newsletter you honor & offer recognition to the existing subscriber of your newsletter who has referred the most new confirmed subscribers to your online newsletter.

Ask the winners for permission to print their names first to protect their privacy.

Consider providing a trophy to the person. Alternatively you can award them an honorary medal, or award certificate.

This is a great way to increase your subscriber count, and also a great way to bring recognition to people who may feel otherwise under appreciated. A win win situation for everyone involved!

Idea # 2

Recognize All Existing Subscribers Who Refer Others

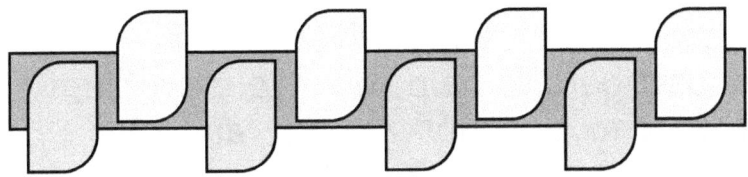

Provide a recognition section of your newsletter which lists the names of every existing subscriber who has referred one or more new subscriber(s) to your newsletter.

You can add a regular section in your newsletter for this purpose, listing the referring subscriber's name, and also can list the number of confirmed subscribers who they referred to your newsletter mailing list in parenthesis.

Ask subscribers for permission to print their names first to protect their privacy.

An example:

    Randall Kowalenko (3)
    John Reader   (2)
    Jane Robertson   (1)
    Cindy Johnson   (1)

Recognition can motivate your subscribers to help solve your problem (not enough subscribers), and also make them aware that you have a problem that they can help solve for you. Remember, people can't help you if they don't know you need help.

Idea # 3

Offer A Secret Prize To Existing Subscribers Who Refer Others

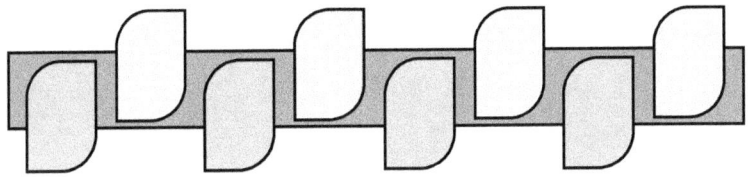

In your newsletter you can offer a special secret prize of value to your subscribers when they get 3 verified friends to subscribe.

Advise them to send you an email with the email addresses of the 3 friends after they have subscribed to your online newsletter. Next, verify that the email addresses are confirmed subscribers to your list.

After verifying the new subscribers have joined you can email a special discount coupon, or other valuable prize to the existing subscriber who referred them to you. Alternatively, if you want them to stop by your office you can give them a copy of a good book. You can buy great new books in bulk for a cheap price at www.tripleclicks.com in the 'On Sale' category.

Idea # 4

Offer Free Promotion To The Top Referring Subscriber

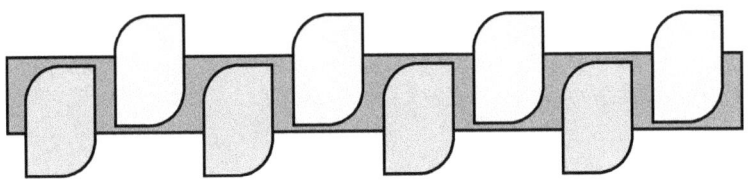

Offer a free promotion in your next newsletter issue for the existing subscriber who refers the most new confirmed subscribers.

You can make a normal advertisement section in your online newsletter just to promote the previous months top referring subscriber.

Make sure that you advertise & explain this free promotion so that your subscribers are aware of your offer, and tell them the dimensions of the free promotion so they don't misunderstand how large of an advertising section they can expect to fill if they win the contest.

If your list is large mention how many subscribers you have as a way to add extra interest to your offer.

Idea # 5

Offer A Free Prize As An Incentive To Join Your Newsletter

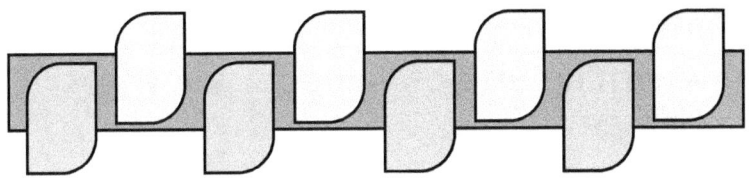

Offer a free prize to everyone who joins your newsletter. Here are a few ideas of what to give:

- Old inventory or surplus stock items

- An e-book you buy PLR rights to (www.theplrstore.com) that you give away free

- A printed book of interest to your subscribers - again, visit www.tripleclicks.com in the 'On Sale' category for cheap new books in quantity

- A mini-course you write

- Video interview which you upload to

your website on a hidden page built just for it

- A recorded audio interview of you & another professional that you upload to your website
- A Video demonstration or training video
- Anything else of value for a low cost or free

Idea # 6

Offer A Monthly Lottery To All Subscribers For A Grand Prize

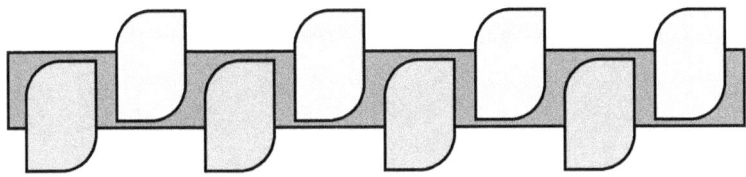

Offer a monthly lottery for a grand prize such as a $50 gift certificate to a nice restaurant, or possibly a coupon for a dinner and a movie for two.

To encourage new subscribers to join - advise clearly in your online newsletter that this lottery is offered exclusively to subscribers and that anyone can join it.

Make sure you provide directions for joining your newsletter to maximize your results.

Offering something like this should spur

some great interest if the prize valuable.

Encourage your subscribers to tell others about this give lottery as well in your online newsletter.

Idea # 7

Offer A Coupon Which Is Redeemable Only By New Subscribers

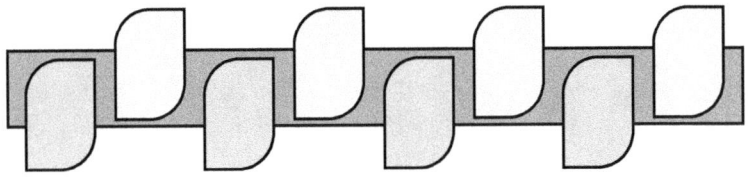

You can offer a discount coupon for your products or services that can only be redeemed by new subscribers to your online newsletter.

You can promote this offer either in your newsletter, on your newsletter signup webpage, or in both places.

Also, to ensure that your existing subscribers don't feel left out you can extend the offer to them if they refer one or more new subscribers to you.

In this scenario both the referring

subscriber and the new subscriber will receive the discount coupon. That way you encourage their participation in your list building efforts in exchange for their eligibility of the coupon reward.

Idea # 8

Offer The Opportunity For New Subscribers To Purchase Discounted Gift Certificates

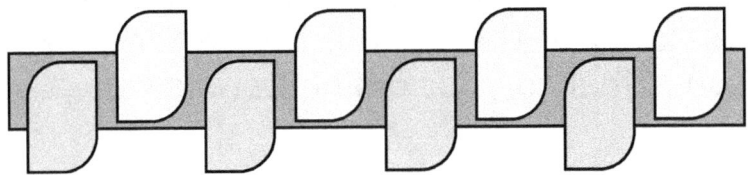

Offer gift certificates for sale at a discounted price for your products or services to new newsletter subscribers only.

If you don't already have company gift certificates and it is not against your companies policies you can even make your own. You can then scan them and email them to reduce mailing expenses & time. Alternatively you can buy them at office supply stores (but I don't suggest copying & scanning them if that is the case to ensure you are not breaking copyright laws).

What's great is that gift certificate money is guaranteed to be spent at your organization instead of one of your competitors.

To ensure your existing subscribers don't feel left out you can consider extending this offer to them too if they refer a new subscriber to your online newsletter.

Idea # 9

**Offer The Opportunity For A Free
Consultation To New Subscribers**

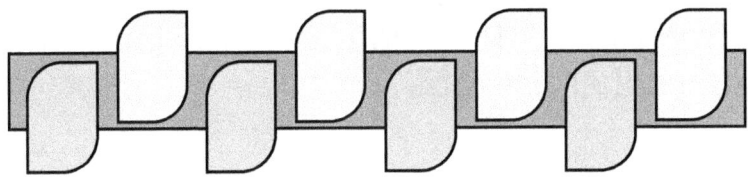

You can offer new subscribers a coupon
for a free consultation. This promotion
can be on your signup webpage and / or
your newsletter.

Mention that anyone can join your online
newsletter to become eligible for the
coupon, and provide directions on how
they can subscribe to it.

Depending on your profession you may
or may not decide to include your
existing subscribers in this offer. If you
work in an industry where your job
depends on you making free

appointments in the first place you can simply extend this offer to those in your existing subscriber list that refer a new subscriber.

Its a great way for contacts to reach you for an appointment instead of you going after them. Plus you are growing your subscriber list too!

Idea # 10

Mention Your Online Newsletter On Your Business Card

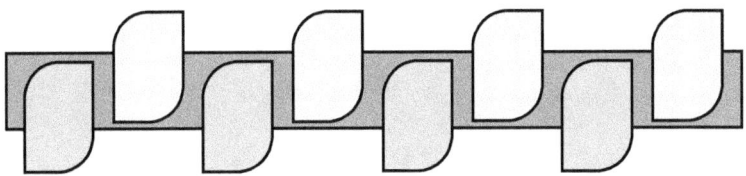

Mention your online newsletter on your business card with instructions on how to subscribe to it.

If you are already buying business cards there shouldn't be any extra cost associated with implementing this idea unless you decide to add the information on the back of a previously one sided business card. Promoting it on the front may save you the costs of printing on the back of the card, but also will provide greater exposure if you are able to squeeze it in.

When you hand out your business card make sure you mention your online newsletter to the recipient and explain that they can sign up for it through the webpage mentioned on it. It's easy to make a habit of mentioning it with practice!

Idea # 11

Create 'Sizzle' Cards Which Promote New Online Newsletter Subscriptions

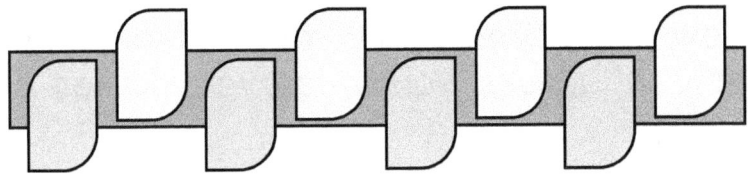

You can create 'Sizzle' cards which encourage & direct people to sign up for your online newsletter - there is even a place where you can get them for free minus the cost of shipping if you are a new customer.

At the time of this writing, an on-going promotion that is and has been offered at Vista Print (www.vistaprint.com) for some time is to provide you with 250 *FREE* Full-Color Business cards which I suggest you essentially make into 'Sizzle' cards to promote your online newsletter instead of putting your name on it.

You will likely need to choose one of Vista Print's forty two design templates that will fit the webpage address for your online newsletter's signup form, and keep it in the center of the business card if possible.

How many times have you met someone new who asks you what you do for a living?

I don't know about you, but I can tell you it happens to me extremely frequently.

This is a great chance to prospect.

Give these cards away to promote your newsletter to everyone you meet who you discuss your online newsletter with.

Idea # 12

Post A Classifieds Ad On Craigslist To Recruit New Subscribers

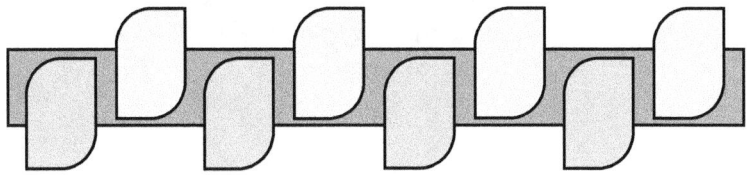

In the world of online advertising its going to be tough to find a more predominate classifieds ad service than Craigslist (www.craigslist.org). In many locations & assorted categories you can even post ads for free at the time of this writing.

If you have never heard of or used Craigslist before you will be glad to hear that there are many people who go there very frequently or daily.

You can create an online classifieds ad promoting your online newsletter by offering a brief, warm introduction to yourself and an overview of what your newsletter covers, and provide directions on how people can subscribe.

Craigslist has categories for states and even many cities so you can target your geographic market if desired!

Idea # 13

Post A Classifieds Ad On eBayClassifieds To Recruit New Subscribers

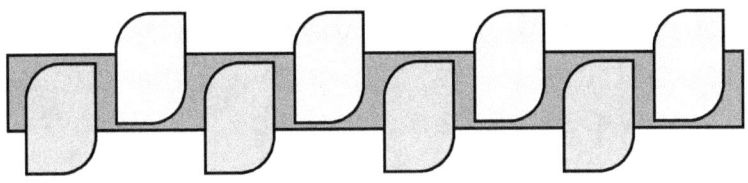

Separate from the primary eBay.com website, eBay offers a free classifieds service (www.ebayclassifieds.com) which is fairly new & also free at the time of this writing.

Since eBay is the parent company for this service it is likely to be around for a long time.

When you go to eBayClassifieds you type in your zip code to ensure you place your ad in your geographic area of influence, or you can enter a different location if desired.

There are also numerous categories.

You can create an online classifieds ad promoting your online newsletter by offering a brief, warm introduction to yourself and an overview of what your newsletter covers, and provide directions on how people can subscribe.

As always, read their terms of service before submitting an ad to ensure it does not violate any of their rules.

Also, to avoid confusion, please note that eBayClassifieds.com is a separate service from the primary eBay.com website which is not free. Idea # 14 will discuss the paid classifieds ads offered on the core eBay.com website.

Idea # 14

Post A Classifieds Ad On eBay To Recruit New Subscribers

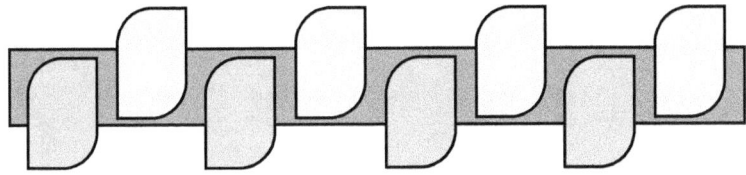

Almost everybody knows you can buy and sell products on eBay at their main website (www.ebay.com), but many people are unaware that you can post a classifieds ad there as well.

In my opinion eBay has some fairly strict rules governing your classifieds ad, and also costs $10 per month at the time of this writing.

With that said, the good side is that eBay is one of the top ranking websites in the world and enjoys a zealous following along with an insane amount of visitor traffic - which may be interested in your online newsletter!

If you setup an eBay classifieds ad make sure you understand their rules first, and consider offering a freebie to those who subscribe.

Idea # 15

Post A Classifieds Ad In The Newspaper To Recruit New Subscribers

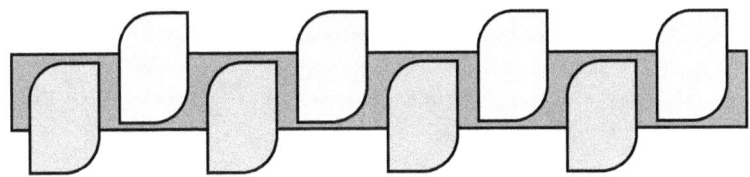

You can post a small classifieds ad in the newspaper to recruit new subscribers to your online newsletter. The Sunday paper is almost always preferred due to it's high circulation.

The drawbacks to this strategy is that it is not free, and secondly you are requesting extra effort on the readers behalf to get up from their chair, go to their computer, login, and visit your signup page.

I highly suggest offering a valuable free incentive to subscribe. The freebie will need to outweigh the extra effort required by the reader to join.

On an encouraging note, readership for many newspapers is very high and geographically targeted.

Idea # 16

During Appointments Ask Clients & Prospects If They Are Interested In Subscribing

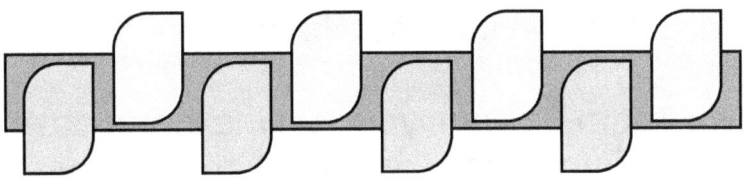

When having meetings or appointments with clients and prospects ask them if they are interested in subscribing to your online newsletter.

You can expect an especially generous signup rate from this strategy. After all, the contact usually would not be spending their precious time to meet with you if they don't have any use for your product or service. It is especially important to ask them during your appointment because they are likely warm or even hot leads for what you are offering, and your online newsletter is likely a topic of interest to them at the point in time.

This strategy is not only free, but as I mentioned, it is HIGHLY effective. You may find yourself forgetting to ask, but after you see how well it works it quickly becomes a systematic habit.

Ask them to join your online newsletter even if you just concluded the business you were seeking from them as they are probably receptive to subscribing, and will likely need or know someone who needs your services in the future.

Idea # 17

Write An Industry Report & Offer It As An Incentive For New Subscribers

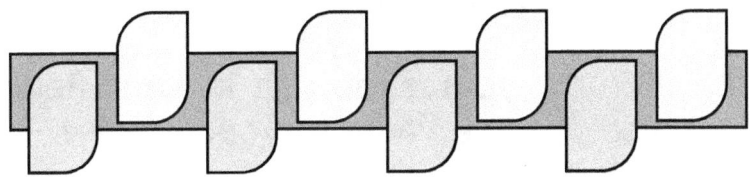

It's likely that you know more about your industry than people who don't work in your field, even if you are a rookie.

So what you can do is write a short interesting industry report then offer it as an incentive for people to join your newsletter subscription. Often the report will have a cover page you can create stating something like:

"The History of Widgets & What Trends You Can Expect In The Future"

You can get a great free word processor

called 'Writer' at www.OpenOffice.org that you can use to both write your guide & save it in .PDF format.

Next you can upload the report to your website and provide new subscribers a link to it when they join.

It will show your expertise in your field and also provide value to your readers.

Idea # 18

Write An Industry Guide & Offer It As An Incentive For New Subscribers

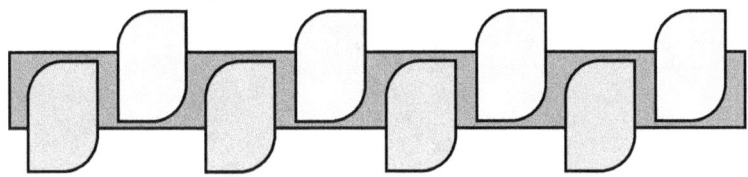

Frequently clients may be uninformed or want further information about how to accomplishing an objective that you specialize in.

What you can do is offer a 5 or 7 step guide that details the ways your clients can accomplish their goal. Examples of guides you could write may be "How To Repair Your Credit In Seven Simple Steps" or "Five Steps To Financial Freedom".

Type the title on the front cover & make it look as professional as possible.

You can get a great free word processor called 'Writer' at www.OpenOffice.org that you can use to both write your guide & save it in .PDF format.

Next you can upload the guide to your website and provide new subscribers a link to it when they join.

Idea # 19

Send A 'Join My Online Newsletter' Flier Out With Products You Sell

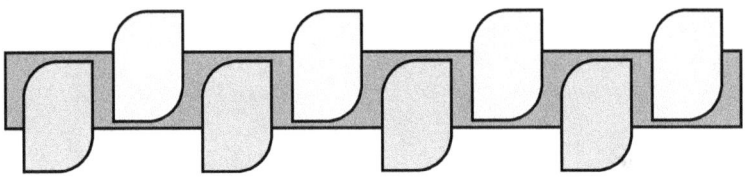

If you send a package or letter out when you sell your products or services, print out fliers which encourage customers to join your online newsletter. You are sending the package or letter anyway, so for the cost of a piece of paper & some ink why not promote your online newsletter too?

Ensure that you provide your signup form's webpage address on the flier, along with additional benefits they can expect to receive from your newsletter. I suggest offering a freebie and mentioning it on your flier as well.

Then whenever you send a package or mail a letter to a non-subscribing customer include the flyer to encourage them to join.

Idea # 20

Publish Your Newsletter Articles On EzineArticles.com

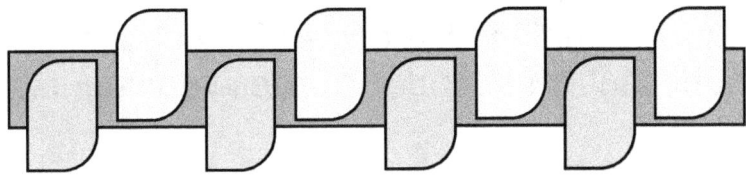

If you are the author of the articles for your newsletter you can submit them for publication on the internet to well know article directories such as EzineArticles (www.ezinearticles.com).

In this arrangement other people with email newsletters, websites and blogs can publish your quality article to their followers too.

At the end of your articles you include a footer that has an advertisement for your online newsletter, and include a link to your signup form's webpage. Then, when others publish your articles EzineArticles requires in their Terms of Service that they also include the promotional footer you created at the bottom along with the rest of the article.

If your article is really good sometimes another mailing list owner may choose to publish it and send it to their mailing list.

They must contain your footer ad you wrote which can drive traffic to your signup form if they are interested in article.

Since you have already written the article why not let others promote you now too!

Idea # 21

Swap Advertisements With Another Newsletter Publisher

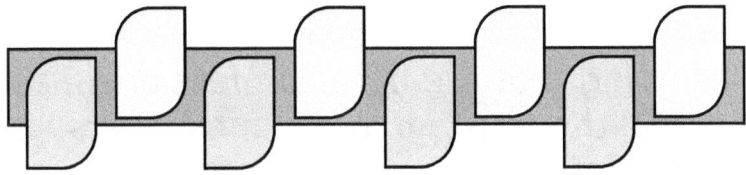

Partnering with another professional who provides a newsletter program for a product or service that compliments yours is a recipe for list building.

You can ask them if they would like to swap ad space in their newsletter in exchange for ad space in your newsletter.

Their product or service should be related but not in direct competition with yours to benefit both parties. You can use the ad space you receive to promote your online newsletter!

You will both need to agree upon the ad size, and the rest is pretty strait forward.

You may decide to do this as an ongoing scheduled arrangement, or choose to only perform an ad swap at certain time intervals.

Assuming that the other professional has gained the trust of their subscribers, it will transfer to your ad as well.

Idea # 22

Seek New Recruits To Your Newsletter At Networking Events

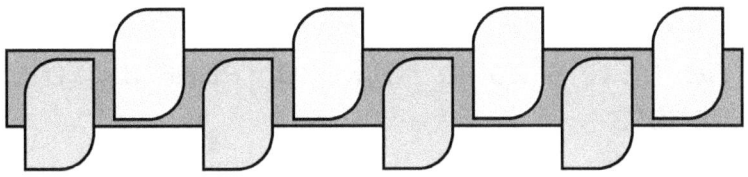

Networking events... Some people love them & can't get enough, while other people hate them... Whether you like or dislike networking events, it is a great chance to promote your online newsletter.

I have been involved with networking events and have found one thing to be pretty true - they are loyal to the other group members.

It seems there are always freebies being given away at these events so I suggest offering a freebie that is tangible for the incentive. You can go to the local networking events in your area, and mention the freebie you are giving to new subscribers & hand out fliers with sign up instructions. The next time the meeting occurs bring the freebies and hand them out to the people who subscribed to your online newsletter.

The next step is to keep repeating the process.

Idea # 23

Start A Local Meetup Group For Your Area Of Expertise

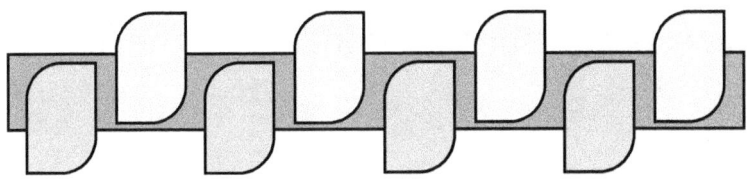

Meetup (www.meetup.com) is a great way to build a group of people sharing a common interest. You can build an online community that meets offline, and schedule group events as well.

You can use this service to build an online group from scratch. You can schedule meetings as desired, & email other members (i.e. so you can promote your newsletter subscription etc.), or even send your online newsletters directly to the other group members by using the 'mailing list' feature.

Meetup is also a great way to meet other professionals in related fields to find new joint venture list building opportunities.

This service is a great way to build a targeted online community, increase business & also promote your online newsletter subscription all at the same time!

Idea # 24

Market Your Online Newsletter To Professional Organizations

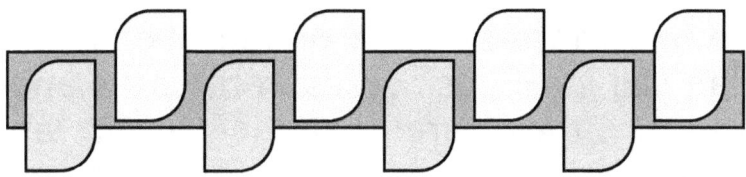

There are professional organizations that have open membership to outside parties which can offer a benefit to their group. Some of these organizations even have networking events. These types of events are an ideal opportunity for you to promote your services as well as your newsletter.

If these groups only meet rarely it is especially recommended to promote your newsletter because the members may otherwise have limited opportunities to develop a personal relationship of trust with you.

If the professional organization has a newsletter for it's members it may be advantageous to find out what is required to place an ad for your newsletter or services in it. As always, offer a freebie if possible.

To find these types of organizations you can call local businesses in the area and see if they are part of such an organization and ask them for the name of the organization and also the contact information if possible.

Idea # 25

Place Brochures In Mailboxes To Promote Your Online Newsletter

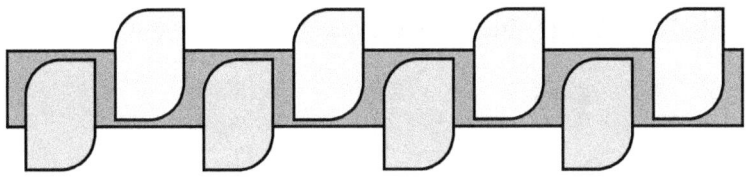

Put a brochure ad for your newsletter in mailboxes of a neighborhood that meets your customers ideal demographic profile.

On the brochure you should provide a warm introduction for yourself, and explain that their location is within your territory and that you wish to service their needs and the needs of their neighbors. Offer your newsletter in a tasteful non-pushy way, and advertise that you will provide them with a free preferably tangible gift for joining.

Often times you will need to repeat this

strategy several times before achieving results as the target neighborhood will not be familiar with you initially.

If possible drop off the tangible gift in person when they subscribe to your newsletter for extra personalization & relationship building.

Idea # 26

Use An External Card Holder On Your Vehicle Promoting Your Online Newsletter

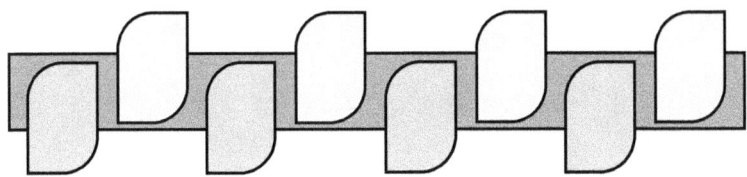

At The Card Box (www.thecardbox.com) you can purchase an external business card holder that you can attach to your vehicle. There are also frequently people offering these items for sale on eBay (www.ebay.com) as well.

You can place business cards that also promote your online newsletter in the card holder, or use sizzle cards which provide a more targeted focus on joining your newsletter subscription.

What's nice about this strategy is that running errands and parking your car aids in your marketing efforts when people take one of your cards.

The only work required on your behalf is mounting the card holder, and refilling it with business cards when it gets low.

Idea # 27

Promote Your Online Newsletter By Teaching An Adult Education Class

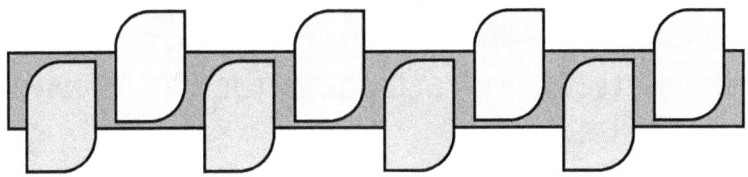

Offering an adult education class locally is a great way to promote not just yourself but your online newsletter too. Attendees will esteem you as an authority after they see how much you know about your area of expertise.

The people who enroll in your class are going to be very highly targeted for your subject matter too. An example would be a Realtor offering a 'For Sale By Owner' course, or an Accountant offering a class on 'How To Do Your Own Small Business Taxes'. Many of the attendees may soon become your future clients if they don't have the time or if they are overwhelmed at performing the task you teach in the class too.

You can also offer other types of courses than the common 'Do It Yourself' style. Regardless of what type of course you decide to offer, promote your online newsletter, and a freebie for those who subscribe.

Some courses even pay you to teach the material, while others you can offer for free!

Idea # 28

Offer A Presentation Swap With A Related Industry Partner's Clientele

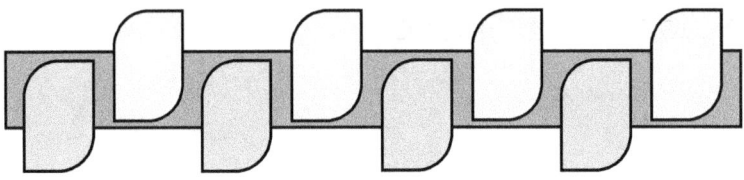

A great way to promote your newsletter is to offer a presentation swap with a professional partner's clients. Both of you can promote the presentation of the other professional in your newsletters, mentioning the date, time and location.

Since likely you will not have recurring encounters with the other professional's clientele I strongly advocate promoting your online newsletter so that you can continue building your relationship with those who attend and establish trust to establish a longer term rapport.

Provide an incentive to join your online newsletter that will enhance your in-person relationship with the subscriber such as a free consultation, or a tangible item that will aid you in scheduling an appointment to deliver it so you can also further discuss the subscribers business needs in your niche.

Idea # 29

Buy A Solo-Mailing Ad To Someone Else's Mailing List

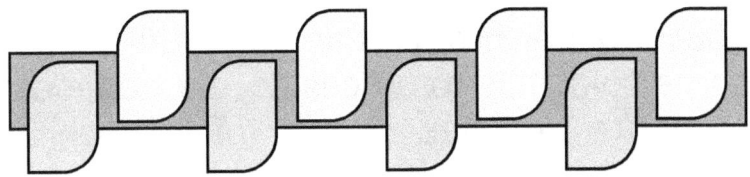

Buying a solo-mailing is another way you can direct people to sign up to your online newsletter. If you work with a professional in a related but not competing field of business that has a decently sized email subscriber list you can ask the owner if you can pay them to run a solo-ad for you. They should run the ad for you to their list, and you should first request written confirmation from the list owner that that their list is spam compliant.

Additionally, you can do a search on the internet using your favorite search engine such as Google, Yahoo or Bing for 'Solo Email Ad' or other similar keywords to find individuals interested in running a solo ad for you.

If you work in a field that requires highly geographically targeted subscribers for your online newsletter you can make some cold calls to offices of related fields to yours and see if they offer such a service or know of someone who might.

I also suggest you familiarize yourself with spam & other laws related to list brokering and solo mailings prior to engaging in this activity to make sure you don't accidentally break any of the applicable laws.

Costs and results vary, but it can be a fast way to grow your list!

Idea # 30

Offer An Advertising Swap With Your Online Newsletter Subscribers

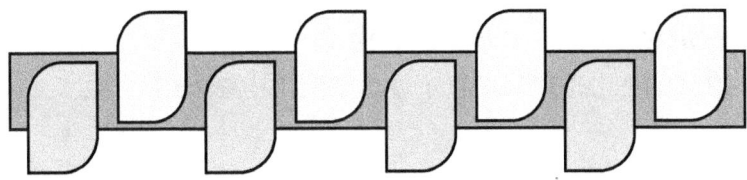

Offer a free advertising section of your newsletter each month where you promote one of your subscribers to the rest of your list in exchange for them promoting your newsletter & services to their clientele or subscriber list.

This strategy would work especially good for reciprocal business fields which compliment your primary specialty such as a Mortgage Loan Officer's relationship to a Real Estate Agent or a Homebuilder.

Some of you subscribers who wish to perform this type of ad swap may have significantly smaller or larger lists than yours, or even no list at all, but may be able to advertise you & your online newsletter in other beneficial ways. Its good to consider some negotiations you can provide when the swap is not even such as the person with the smaller list promote your ad three times in exchange for one promotion on your behalf etc.

Its good to keep as many ad swap opportunity options as possible open, just make sure that before you make the offer have some creative negotiations to accommodate those who have more and less value to provide in the exchange.

Be flexible and this can be a great way to joint venture with others.

Idea # 31

Barter Your Product or Service In Exchange For Promoting Your Online Newsletter

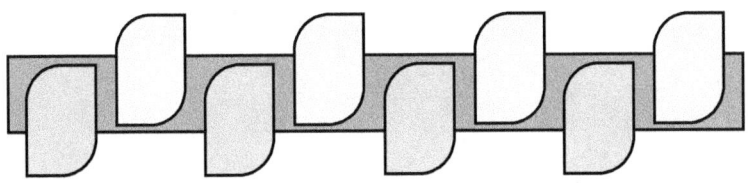

If you can cheaply acquire or provide the product or service that you offer then you may consider offering it as a freebie or a barter to other professionals that can promote your list.

This arrangement is best offered to professionals in other industries which are related to yours where your marketing will be most effective since there may be product or service expenses involved.

In some businesses it can be a great exchange, and if it isn't then perhaps it may not be worth the loss to employ this arrangement. Regardless, it is a great way to promote your online newsletter that many people may find very beneficial.

Idea # 32

Write Newsletters For Related Businesses Which Contain An Ad For Your Online Newsletter

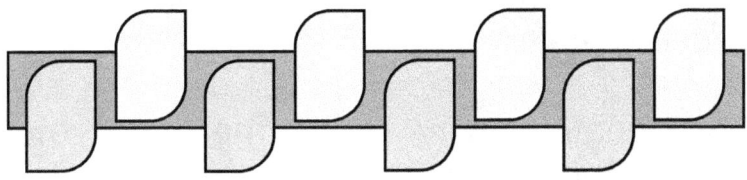

You can write a newsletter for one or more related industry companies that are not your competitors. It should include an ad to join your newsletter every month - especially if the related company does not already have a newsletter and if they have a large list.

For instance, if you work as a Mortgage Loan Officer you may want to find a well renowned Real Estate Agent in your area who does not already provide an online newsletter to their clientele. You can offer to write them a monthly online newsletter for free if they agree to allow you to advertise yourself and your online newsletter in every issue.

Since this is a related industry you can likely use many of the articles you wrote for your own newsletter in the one you make for them, which will make it go much quicker.

Additionally, why not improve your results by providing the same newsletter that you made for the first Real Estate Agent to other Real Estate agents with large client bases too?

The other professional may be hesitant to offer a paper version of a newsletter to their clientele due to printing and mailing costs, so encourage them to provide it to their client base via blast email service which is very affordable. Additionally, if it is offered via email subscribers will be at their computers already so it will be less trouble for them to go to your signup form and join than if they were reading it on paper.

Idea # 33

Advertise Your Online Newsletter On Public Access Television

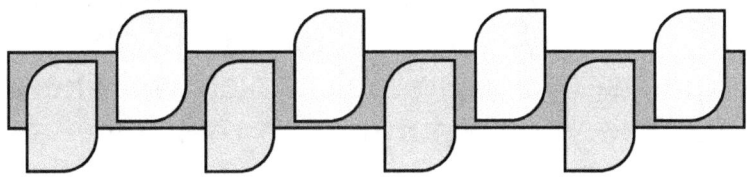

You may be able to advertise your online newsletter as well as yourself on Public Access Television. First, however, you need to understand the terms, conditions and guidelines of the public access provider to ensure that your promotion will not violate any of their rules. Especially make sure that business marketing is allowed first.

You can offer training lesson sessions on your online newsletter's topic & provide information on how the viewers can reach you in person and how they can join your online newsletter.

If you decide to use this method of promotion I strongly suggest making it as appealing and interesting as possible. Also, don't forget that people like humor if appropriate with your theme.

The viewers who watch your broadcast will quickly see your authority & expertise on your topic which will likely increase your reputation in their eyes as a result.

If you demonstration is a live broadcast you can likely provide a hotline number for people to reach you and ask you questions right on the spot!

Idea # 34

Twist Clown Balloons & Hand Out Your Sizzle Or Business Cards

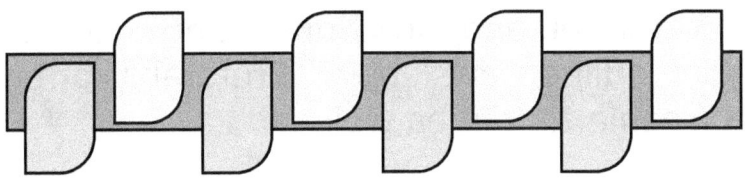

This idea is a bizarre one! I still recall riding the Chicago subway one evening on my way to a date. There was a gentleman who was twisting clown balloons for kids for a dollar or two.

While I never pursued the idea any farther I thought of how great of a way that would be to market to my territory.

The idea could go something like this: Go to a busy intersection or area of town where there will be kids accompanied by their parents. Then offer to twist them a balloon for free - offer them a few choices (balloon animal, balloon flower, balloon crown etc) and let them choose the colors you have available.

Then twist the balloon, and provide it to the child, and provide the parent a sizzle card or business card with your contact information and directions on how to join your online newsletter. Preferably offer a freebie to join as well.

I don't suggest dressing up like a clown as you don't want to scare the kids etc, but you can still make a very lasting & original impression. In fact I even bought a balloon flower for my date from the man on the subway.

Be up-beat & friendly and as crazy as this idea may sound you should get some pretty memorable exposure.

You may first need to buy a training kit on eBay or elsewhere which provides balloons & video instruction to help you get started. Have fun!

Idea # 35

Use Twitter Marketing To Find Other Experts's Customers In Your Area

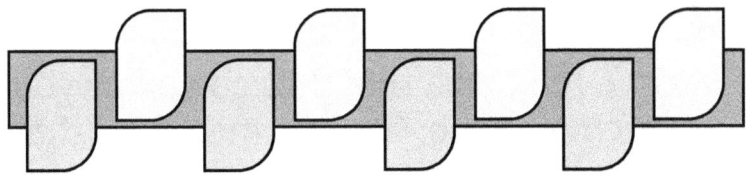

Twitter, Twitter, Twitter - that name seems to pop up all the time in the last couple of years.

While it's true that many people use Twitter for social purposes, there are other people who use it for business related purposes.

At the time of this writing I have over 12,000 'followers' (people who subscribe to the information that I post), and I provide some great information on the topic of newsletters.

What's great is you can start a Twitter account on the topic of your online newsletter, provide quality information to your readers, and even promote your online newsletter to them - all they have to do is click on the link you broadcast and they can sign up.

Twitter even has a tool that can allow you to search for other Twitter members that match the demographic criteria you enter. You can even search by a certain distance from a location. Their search tool is located at:

http://search.twitter.com/advanced

You can search for other related professionals on Twitter (even in your area if you choose), then 'follow' (become the friend of) all of their followers. Twitter etiquette is that you follow back people who follow you, so many of the people you follow will likely follow you back. Then you can promote your online newsletter & offer interesting industry information to them.

Idea # 36

Use Facebook To Market Your Online Newsletter

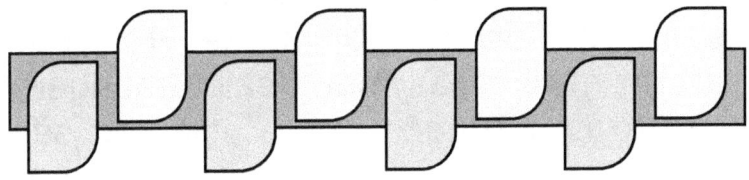

You can market your online newsletter using the 'Facebook' service. You can sign up for a Facebook account at:

http://www.facebook.com

Then you can find previous classmates colleagues long lost friends and more to promote your online newsletter to. You can even start a group on the topic of your online newsletter which people all over the world can join if they find it interesting.

In your profile you can also promote

your online newsletter.

One thing to keep in mind is that many of the people who join your Facebook 'friends' list will likely be people who you know, and may be turned off by an overly aggressive marketing campaign. So if you decide to market to your 'natural market' as many sales mangers refer to it, I suggest more of a soft sell approach - otherwise you may irritate or alienate yourself from them.

Facebook has a very large following and is very popular.

Idea # 37

Use LinkedIn To Promote Your Online Newsletter

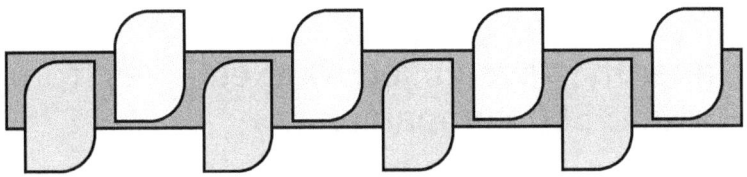

LinkedIn is a popular online networking community that specifically caters to business professionals.

You can sign up for LinkedIn at:

http://www.linkedin.com/

Linked in is a great platform for business people to network with others, where you can even create an online community similar to many of the other online social networking websites.

This service is an excellent way to

promote both your online newsletter as well as yourself.

Additionally, you can establish yourself from a business standpoint by using the Question & Answer board where you and other members can participate.

LinkedIn is even used by executives from Fortune 500 companies.

It's a great place & way of networking online to promote yourself as well as your online newsletter.

Idea # 38

Use The MySpace Community To Promote Your Online Newsletter

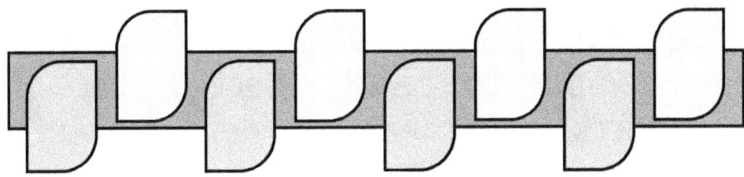

While MySpace isn't the most recent online social networking community it's still a very large one and shouldn't be overlooked just because it isn't the new kid on the block.

You can sign up for a free MySpace account at:

http://www.myspace.com

One interesting note worth mentioning about MySpace (which is the reason that made me decide to add this MySpace marketing idea to this book) is that you can invite an entire large community of people to be your friends from scratch who you don't even know. If you search for a particular demographic and find thousands of results - you can invite them one by one to join your community (be your friend). They might not all accept your friend invitation, but it's nice to be able to hand select a list of prospects who meet the demographics you are seeking instead of just friends who you know etc.

I recommend that you grow your friends community slowly but surely each week as your account can be blocked if you request too many friends in too short of a time period.

You can also create groups that others can join. You can promote your online newsletter to your MySpace friends & groups, although I recommend offering quality information too, and suggest a soft selling approach.

Idea # 39

**Design Free Newsletter Templates
For Others To Use That Promote
Your Online Newsletter**

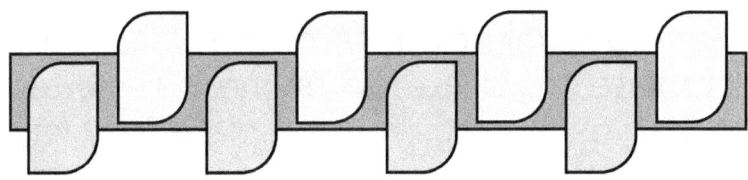

If you design your own newsletter using PDF design software then why not make some free templates that others can use to build their newsletter? You can simply give away the templates which you have already created, and offer them to your subscribers to use for the newsletters they write. But keep reading...

The catch is that you need to provide a link to your newsletter signup form in one of the corners, where you type something like '*Free Template Provided By Randall Kowalenko*'. When you offer your templates to others, ensure that you advise publicly that the templates are available for free use and can be edited and changed in any way desired as long as your personalized link ad is unaltered and left included on the finished newsletter.

That way whenever someone uses your template to create an online newsletter of their own using your template they will be indirectly promoting your newsletter to their subscribers as well.

The PDF design software that I use and recommend is PagePlus, and can be purchased at:

http://www.serif.com/pageplus/

While on that topic, feel free to visit my website to use or see my free templates to get ideas for making some of your own at:

http://www.randallkowalenko.com/

Idea # 40

Make A YouTube Video Series On The Topic Of Your Online Newsletter

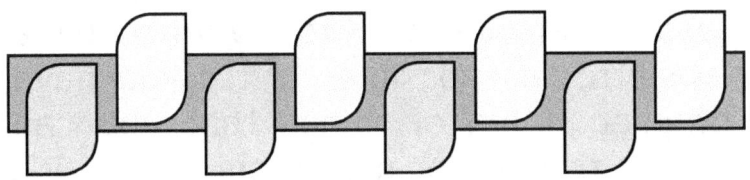

YouTube is one of the highest traffic websites in the world. And the great part is that you can benefit from their success for free. Viewers can even spread the link to your videos!

To sign up for free, visit:

http://www.youtube.com

It's good to have a user name that reflects the topic of your online newsletter. Also, make certain that you fill out your profile description, provide the link to your webpage with your newsletter signup form, and whatever other information you would like to add. Also, don't forget to upload a picture of yourself.

In order to maximize your results I suggest making a list of as many video ideas that relate to your online newsletter as possible. After you have compiled a list of things that you can provide training or mentorship about it's time to start making the videos.

You can use a webcam from your computer, or even a video from your cell phone if someone else can film you and the quality is good enough.

I suggest naming the video three words or less if possible, and make the name as closely related to what the video is about as possible.

YouTube marketing best suits people who are looking for global subcribers instead of just the local area.

Idea # 41

Use Industry Forums To Promote Your Online Newsletter

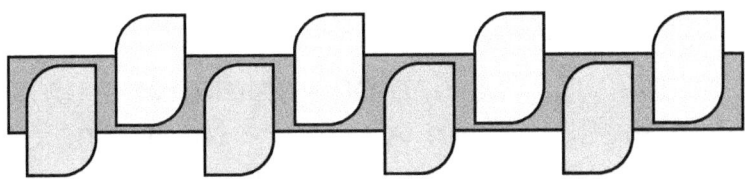

There are an abundance of industry forums on the internet, and you can use them to promote your online newsletter.

There are far too many topics of online newsletters to make a concise list of the best forums for you, but it isn't usually to hard to find one (or several) you're looking for.

Simply go to Google:

http://www.google.com

and search for your newsletter's topic by

simply typing the topic of your online newsletter and attach the word 'forum' after it, then press the 'Google Search' button.

Example of what to type in the search field: Investing Forum

Usually you will find one or many forums of interest. When you join a forum make sure you update your profile, and add a link to the signup page for your online newsletter.

Usually it's good to ease into the forum so that other members don't feel defensive with your posts coming out of nowhere all of a sudden. And I wouldn't suggest being very aggressive in your sales approach either.

Additionally, different forums have different rules about promoting & advertising, so read their Terms of Service when you join. If the forums rules are too strict you may consider finding a more easygoing one.

Idea # 42

Use Viral Documents To Promote Your Online Newsletter

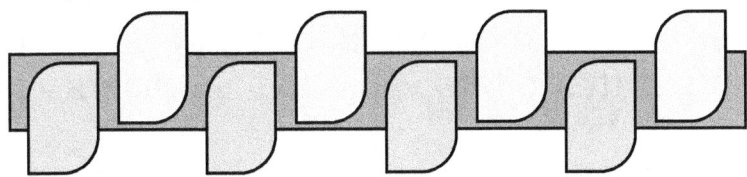

What's a viral report? It's a report that you can give away to people who visit your website or to your subscribers that they can in turn give away for free to their own subscribers & others with the condition that they are not allowed to edit the content.

With this technique you can use a free word processor such as the 'Writer' application in the OpenOffice suite to create a PDF document which offers value to your readers (a guide, a report, tips, instructions etc) and promotes your online newsletter.

You can download the OpenOffice suite for free at:

http://www.openoffice.org

After downloading and installing this wonderful free software package, you can make a short document of your choice that offers value to it's readers.

I suggest adding a cover page to make it look as professional as possible.

When making your report, there are two things you should include - preferably as early as possible in the report:

• Instructions on how & where readers can sign up for your online newsletter

• A statement that your document can be given away for free if the content is unaltered

It's best to make these reports short so you can produce as many as possible.

Idea # 43

Use Scribd To Promote Your Online Newsletter

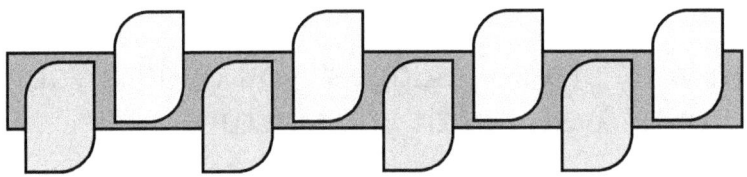

Using viral documents to promote your online newsletter is a great idea, but what if you don't receive much traffic to your website to promote them to the masses?

Additionally, if you have only a small subscriber list to provide your viral report to, or want to increase your exposure how can you do it?

One very popular way to promote your free viral document through a high traffic website is by using Scribd.

Scribd is not only free for you to use to promote your free documents, but it also enjoys millions of web hits each month.

You can visit Scribd's website at:

http://www.scribd.com/

In your profile I suggest you update your profile Avatar with your picture.

What's great is that other members who like your material can subscribe to your account to keep them aware of new information you are providing.

You can send messages to & receive messages from other members as well.

Additionally, Scribd provides a link to your document that people can spread to others. They can also download the document so they can post it on their website or offer it as an email attachment etc.

Idea # 44

Promote Your Online Newsletter Using PodCasting

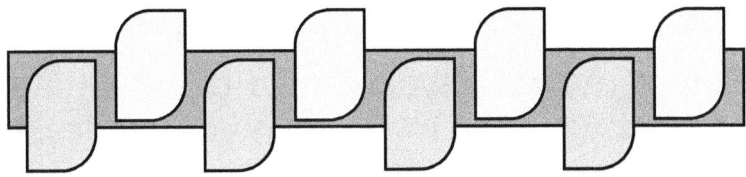

Podcasting is simply a form of audio broadcasting in which your listening audience can download your broadcast and listen to it on their computer, MP3 player or similar listening device.

Podcasting is not as familiar of a form of broadcasting as many of the other more highly publicized forms of communication, but regardless there is a strong, devout following to these broadcasts by many who listen to them.

If you have a computer, a microphone, or even a cell phone that can record and produce your broadcast you can start one of your own. Podcast Alley is a very popular free podcast directory that you can use to upload & share your podcast. Their web address is:

http://www.podcastalley.com/

Before recording you can write an outline of what you plan to cover in your podcast. Don't forget to include an advertisement for your online newsletter.

To develop a following for your podcast make it as interesting as you can, add personality and possibly a little humor. Make your program consistent each episode, and consider using guest speakers who you converse with so its more of a free conversation than an announcement. Provide consistency with the delivery schedule and length of the broadcast. If you promote your podcast as being offered every Monday at noon for half an hour then follow through or your following will decrease.

Idea # 45

Promote Your Online Newsletter And Earn Money By Writing A Book

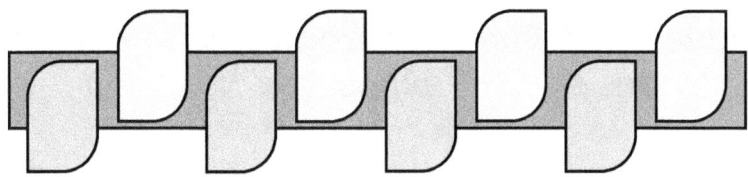

In online marketing whether you are promoting newsletters or widgets, you may have noticed that writing is involved with many of the free and low cost strategies presented.

If you are on an especially tight budget, you can write a book and mention your online newsletter in it. Keep in mind it is a book & not a marketing publication, but there is no reason you can't mildly promote your online newsletter if it is not an overwhelming focus of the book.

You can self-publish it through

CreateSpace, which is an Amazon.com company. Visit CreateSpace at:

http://www.createspace.com

What's great about publishing through CreateSpace is that your book is advertised on Amazon.com - which provides a lot of exposure.

It is free to publish your book, although you will need to buy the first copy of it as a proof to ensure it looks right. You are paid a royalty for each copy sold based on the sales revenue & sales expenses. You can even take your profits to pay for your online newsletter's marketing budget.

First, write down what chapters you will need, after that write the sub headings that need to be discussed, then finally, write what you want to say about each of the sub headings.   Don't forget to mention your online newsletter in your book and provide a website address to your signup form. Your book is written!

Idea # 46

Promote Your Online Newsletter Using Brochures

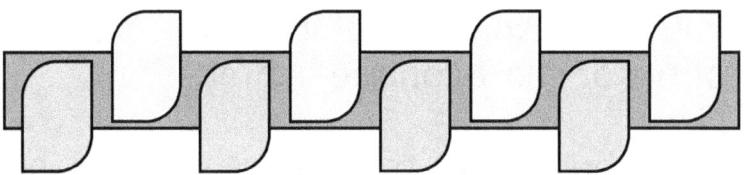

You can market your online newsletter by creating a brochure which you post in your local libraries, grocery stores, laundromats and other local locations.

If you do not already have software which you can use to design brochures you can use the 'Presentation' application which is part of the free OpenOffice software suite. You can download it free at:

http://www.openoffice.org

When you design your brochure create

little vertical tabs at the bottom with your contact information on them & the web address of your online newsletter's signup form.

In the main text use large fonts with eye catching colors. Don't use too much text or people won't read it. Just make a couple of short concise sentences.

At the bottom of the main text area be sure to post the website address to your online newsletter as well as your contact information to ensure that people can write down the information on their own if all of the tabs along the bottom have been taken.

Idea # 47

Invite Existing Clients Not Already Subscribed To Your Online Newsletter To Join

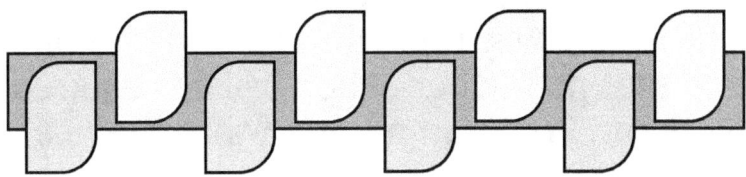

When you start an online newsletter after you have established a significant clientele it's a good idea to invite them to join your newsletter if they have not already subscribed.

It needs to be strongly noted, however, that you should first call your contacts to invite them instead of just manually sending them an email opt-in request to subscribe to your online newsletter. The reason that I mention this is that if they are not expecting your email they will likely consider it to be a spam message. While many of the existing clients you call will be interested in joining your newsletter not all of them will want to.

When they are interested in subscribing to your online newsletter let them know that you will be sending them an email confirmation message with a verification link in it. Ask them to click on the link and that no further action will be required by them. You can mention that they can unsubscribe at any time.

I suggest offering a freebie as well that you mention to your customers before you ask them if they are interested in subscribing.

Regardless, your results should yield a much higher subscription rate if you call them in advance. Also it's good to note that whether they want to join your newsletter or not the phone call will aid in providing a reason to speak with your customers & prospects to further build your relationship with them.

Idea # 48

Setup A Press Release To Promote Your Online Newsletter

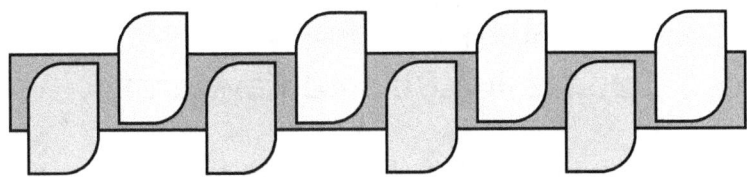

The media is always hungry for new information - it is what ensures their existence & their paychecks.

You can submit a press release that promotes your online newsletter and yourself.

There are numerous press release businesses available which offer different levels of service and pricing.

If you have never issued a press release before you will need to prepare several items before you can make your submission. Some of the items you will need to provide are likely to include:

- A Headline
- A Summary
- The News Body
- The Industry
- The Country
- Submission Related Keywords

As mentioned, there are free to expensive services available. To find the press release package that is most suitable for your needs simply go to Google:

http://www.google.com

And enter a search term into the search box such as: free press release

Simply look through the options until you find the service that is most appropriate for your needs.

Idea # 49

Promote Your Online Newsletter Using Yahoo Answers

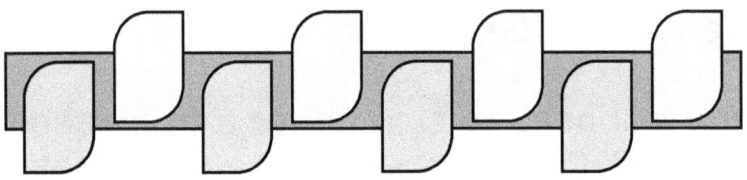

The 'Answers' service provided by Yahoo is a great place to both help people and promote your online newsletter at the same time.

Yahoo Answers is where people can go if they have a specific question that they want to ask - of if they have answers to peoples questions.

In essence, it is an open discussion question and answer session. There are a wide range of categories available where you can either ask questions or provide answers.

You can visit the Yahoo Answers service at:

http://answers.yahoo.com/

Not only is it free to use, but it's also a great way to promote your online newsletter too.

You will need to sign up for a free Yahoo account first if you do not already have one.

Then find questions using the category menu or search fields that relate to the topic of your newsletter. At the bottom of your answer be sure to include a link to one of your webpages that has your online newsletter signup form on it.

Idea # 50

Promote Your Online Newsletter At Flea Markets

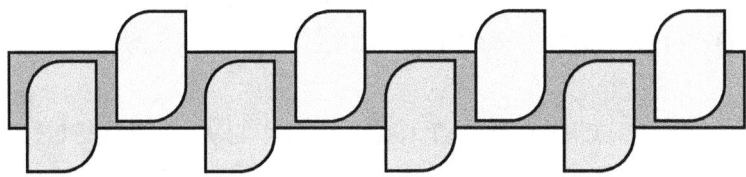

People love flea markets. And even more, they love good deals at flea markets. This is another way you can promote your services and your online newsletter.

You can rent a merchant section, where you promote your services as well as your online newsletter.

You will likely need to bring your own fold out table, and I suggest bringing a transparent bowl which you fill with candy or wrapped chocolates. You will need to bring a stack of business cards. Also, DON'T forget your pen and a tablet of paper.

Place the candy or chocolates that you bought on the table in the bowl you brought. When people stop by to grab a piece of candy you can start talking with them about your profession and how you may be able to service their needs.

If the prospect sounds slightly interested mention your newsletter to them, and ask if you can send them a confirmation link to it. Mention that you are giving away a free book or other freebie (preferably tangible) when someone subscribes through your confirmation link. Write down the names, phone numbers & email addresses of interested prospects. Manually enter their email addresses into your blast email service when you get home so it will send them a confirmation link. If they subscribe to your online newsletter make an appointment to deliver the tangible freebie in person, where you can talk to them at greater depth about their business needs as well.

Idea # 51

Use An Access Password To Encourage New Subscriptions

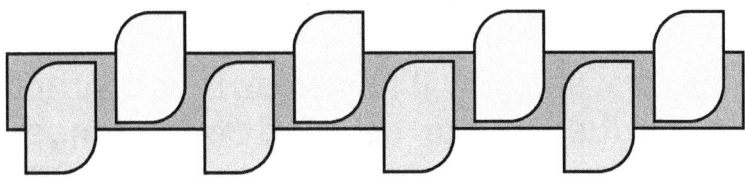

Encourage new subscriptions to your online newsletter by setting up a password protected area on your website where only subscribers can access.

You can mention on your website that presently you are offering free access to the members only area of your website, and that all that they need to do to gain instant access is subscribe to your online newsletter through the subscription form.

When they sign up & confirm their subscription setup a follow up message to send them an email with the current password. You can even update the password each time you release a new issue of your online newsletter. In this case you can provide the new password to your subscribers each time you send out an email to notify them of your new newsletter on your website.

If your website will have less text content on it (due to your newsletters no longer being provided on a webpage accessible to the search engines) you may receive less traffic as a result. So it may be a good idea to also include extra non-newsletter content to your website each month to compensate for this loss. Another idea would be to possibly provide text versions of your old newsletters to the public area of your website with a several month delay.

Idea # 52

Promote Your Online Newsletter By Receiving Testimonials

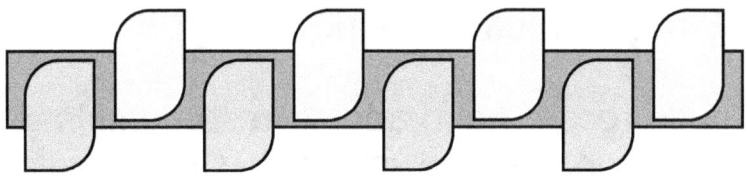

With so many unethical business scams that exist today people want reassurance & proof that results backup your claims. Which is good for your online newsletter & business in general if you have satisfied clients or subscribers.

Whenever you have a client who is extremely appreciative or overwhelmed by your outstanding service and assistance simply ask them for a testimonial. Mention that you may use it on your website, in your newsletters, or other marketing materials.

When you receive the testimonial you can post it (along with their first name and city) on your website by rewriting it word for word. Post it on your signup webpage preferably above or next to the signup form, along with numerous other testimonials if possible. Add a lot of them if you have them.

I also recommend adding testimonials to your online newsletter since your subscribers can spread it to others. You can add them in their own reserved section of your newsletter. Not only can testimonials assist in acquiring new subscribers, but can also aid in retaining existing ones.

Using testimonials will help to increase your credibility, which will also help to instill prospective subscribers with a greater level of trust and confidence in your professional abilities & experience.

Idea # 53

Add A Signup Form To Every Page Of Your Website

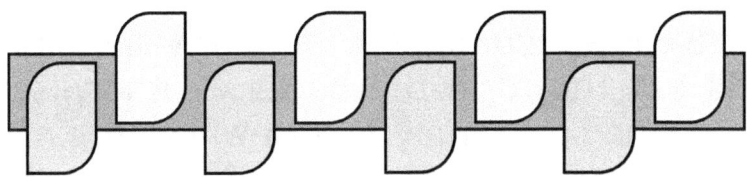

If you are using a website to acquire subscribers for your online newsletter you can add a signup form to not just the primary signup webpage, but to every page on your website.

Adding a signup form to all of your webpages usually doesn't require that much work to do. You just simply copy the form and paste the html on each of the pages of your website.

It's just normal for most people to take the path of least resistance. That's why you should do whatever you can to reduce the effort that is required of your website visitors in order to fill out your subscription form. If they have to hunt for your subscription form on their own they may get distracted, become lazy, or simply forget to look for it on their own.

The easier you make it for your visitors to fill out the form the better. Otherwise the web surfer may go elsewhere to find the information they seek - possibly to one of your competitors who makes their sign up form easier to find!

Idea # 54

Market Your Online Newsletter By Adding An 'About Us' Webpage

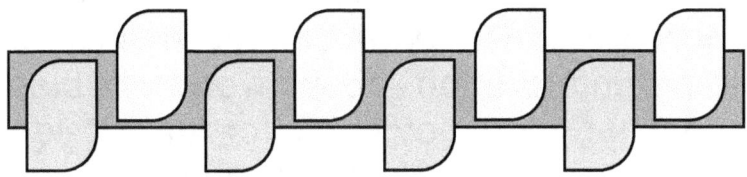

You can assist in your online newsleter marketing efforts by promoting your credibility through the use of an 'About Us' section on your website.

One significant factor that deters prospective subscribers from joining your newsletter is trust.

It's hard for a website visitor to trust someone they have never met, who is mysterious with no known personality.

If you add an 'About Us' webpage to your website you can begin to build a relationship with the visitors to your web-site.

Some information you can add to your 'About Us' page would include your name, your location, your experience, a story that discusses how you came to be in your profession, you can even include some information about your hobbies and what you enjoy doing for fun outside of work. Add a little personality.

Adding this information helps to lower the defenses of someone who otherwise has no reason to trust you, which increases their chances of subscribing to your online newsletter or doing business with you.

One additional thing to mention is that many SEO (Search Engine Optimization) experts claim that adding an 'About Us' page helps raise your website's search engine ranking.

Idea # 55

Provide Your Employees With Sizzle Cards To Promote Your Online Newsletter

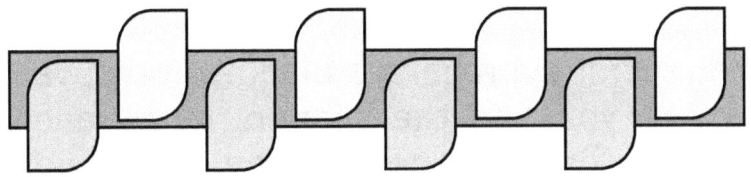

If you have employees you can multiply your efforts to promote your online newsletter by providing them with sizzle cards to hand out to others.

If you have employees who work for you they meet and run into individuals all the time who inquire about their livelihood. Some of your personnel may offer to help promote your online newsletter by giving sizzle cards to people who they meet or know.

For every employee that hands out your sizzle cards it is a leveraged way to expand your influence beyond what you can do on your own.

You can even setup some friendly group competition where you offer a prize each month to the employee who has the highest number of confirmed subscribers to your online newsletter.

You might even hang a plaque on the wall where you add the winners name each month, or find another way to provide recognition to them such as buying a trophy for your office that they get to keep at their cube until they are dethroned by another colleague for having the most monthly subscriber referrals in a one month time period.

Idea # 56

Conduct A Survey And Provide The Results In Your Online Newsletter

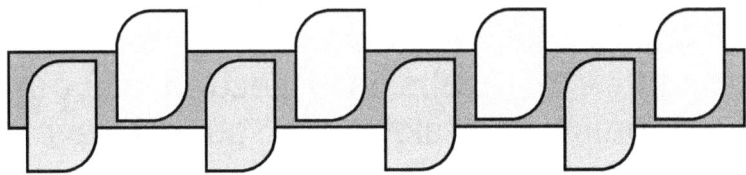

You can conduct a survey to encourage new subscribers to your online newsletter.

Some blast email services offer you the ability to develop a survey, and then produce a link or snippet of HTML code that you can paste onto your website which will track & provide you with the survey's results.

You can make the survey publicly available to everyone who visits your website, but only provide the results in your online newsletter then provide instructions on how people can join it.

I recommend mentioning the cut-off date as well as details on how and when you plan to share the results so interested participants can know what to expect.

Then you can send either a broadcast email which provides the results or if it is a less time sensitive topic you can provide the results in a section of your next online newsletter. You can even offer a survey every month and have a special section of your online newsletter dedicated exclusively to providing the survey results each issue.

Idea # 57

Promote Your Online Newsletter With An Easy To Remember Domain Name

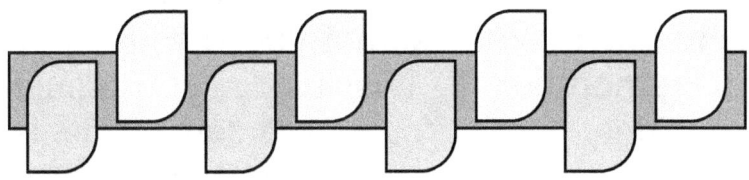

Promoting your online newsletter using an easy to remember domain name can mean the difference between people remembering and forgetting your website.

It's happened to almost all of us at one time or another. You unexpectedly meet someone who is interested in your product, your service, or your online newsletter but you don't have any business cards with you...

Often a napkin or a text message can suffice, but it's also good to have an easy to remember website address that you can tell people verbally as well. It also looks professional on your business & sizzle cards.

Don't get me wrong, any domain name is far better than having no web presence at all, but since you need to have one why not make it something that is easy to remember if possible. You could consider using YourName.com if it is available, or something else that's catchy and easy to remember.

Just consider the two below domain names:

'www.zoaty.com'

www.serversareus26897.com/zoaty

Which one looks more professional and like a business you would prefer to do business with? The top choice would likely be my preference. Normally you can usually register a domain name for under $20 per year!

Idea # 58

Promote Your Online Newsletter By Including A Footer Signature To Your Emails

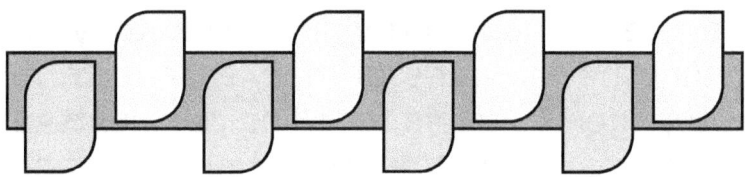

You can use email that you send out to promote your online newsletter by using a signature in the footer of the messages you send out.

This is an excellent free way to promote your online newsletter with little effort by attaching a few words of text to an email you are sending regardless. If your going to send the email anyway, why not get a little extra promotion for your online newsletter?

Many email services provide you the option of attaching an automatic signature so you only need to set it up once and not keep retyping you footer message at the bottom of your email every time.

In your message you can include a short promotional message for your online newsletter, and provide a link to your online newsletter's primary signup form webpage. To avoid repelling recipients of your email keep the promotion short and sweet using only one or two short sentences and your sign up link.

An example of a footer message could be something like:

'Times are changing and so are the interest rates! Stay ahead of the game by subscribing to my monthly mortgage newsletter today at www.domain.com.'

Make your footer message as interesting, catchy, and provocative as possible in the short space you use.

Idea # 59

Promote Your Online Newsletter By Speaking At Conferences & Events

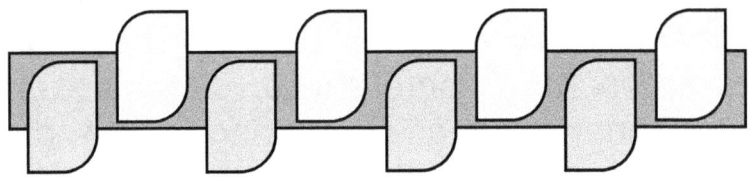

Offering to be a guest speaker at conferences, seminars or other events for related industries is a great way to get exposure for your online newsletter.

An example might be for an occasion where there is continuing education or even large events where there will be a attentive audience for an industry related to yours.

If you can find such an event, know your profession well, and aren't afraid of public speaking in front of groups you can use this opportunity to market your online newsletter and possibly even make some money for your presentation.

To find out about such conferences, first consider industries which are related to yours which are not in direct competition. Next, contact some local professionals in that industry and ask them if they are aware of any conferences, seminars or any other type of continuing education training events that are occurring in the upcoming months. Write down the information they provide you, and then contact the organization offering the event to see if they would be interested in providing you a time slot to speak to their audience about a relevant topic consistent with the other information presented. If there is no room in their schedule you can ask if your speaking involvement would be possible in a future event. Develop a detailed outline for your presentation. At the end of your delivery mention your online newsletter, and how they can join. Don't forget to bring plenty of business or sizzle cards!

Idea # 60

Promote Your Online Newsletter By Leaving Testimonials

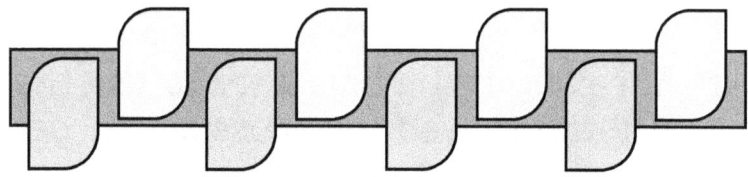

Providing testimonials can often be used to advertise not just for the seller but for the product buyer as well.

Whenever you buy an online product related to your industry you can provide a testimonial to gain promotion for your online newsletter.

There are many websites which even offer the option to leave your testimonial right on the product page (amazon.com comes to mind)

Some such testimonials allow you to

leave a footer, or let you setup a profile in which you can provide a link to your website address where people can sign up for your online newsletter. If you are not allowed to leave a promotional link then move on and find another website that will allow you to.

When leaving testimonials try to use the highest traffic websites possible to get the greatest level of exposure for your efforts.

Some websites don't even require you to order the specific product through their company in order to leave a review for it. In this case to save money you can go to the library, and rent multiple best sellers in your industry. After you read them you can write testimonial reviews for the books that showcase your intelligence and experience as well as possible. Don't forget to include a link to your newsletter signup form in the footer or in your profile. You can repeat this process for as many books in your industry as you like - read then review!

INDEX

cheap, 20, 23
cheaply, 75
Chicago, 81
child, 82
chocolates, 113, 114
choice, 98, 128
choices, 81
choose, 36, 54, 56, 82, 84
Cindy, 18
circulation, 43
cities, 38
city, 118
claim, 122
claims, 117
Class, 67
class, 67, 68
Classifieds, 37, 39, 41, 43
classifieds, 37, 39, 40, 41, 42, 43
classmates, 85
clear, 13
clearly, 25
click, 84, 108
client, 78, 117
Clientele, 69
clientele, 69, 73, 77, 78, 107
Clients, 45, 107
clients, 45, 49, 67, 69, 107, 117
close, 11
closely, 94

Clown, 81
clown, 81, 82
code, 39, 125
cold, 72
colleague, 124
colleagues, 85
Color, 35
colors, 82, 106
com, 20, 23, 35, 39, 40, 41, 53, 59, 65, 84, 85, 87, 89, 92, 93, 95, 100, 102, 104, 110, 112, 128, 130, 133
come, 12
Comes, 11
comes, 10, 133
coming, 96
common, 59, 68
communication, 101
Community, 89
community, 59, 60, 87, 89, 90
companies, 29, 77, 88
company, 29, 39, 77, 104, 134
compensate, 116
competing, 71
competition, 55, 124, 132
competitors, 30, 77, 120
compiled, 94
compliant, 71
compliment, 73
compliments, 55

recorded, 24
recording, 102
Recruit, 37, 39, 41, 43
recruit, 43
Recruits, 57
recurring, 69
Redeemable, 27
redeemed, 27
reduce, 29, 120
Refer, 17, 19
refer, 27, 30, 32, 86
reference, 13
Referrals, 15
referrals, 124
referred, 15, 17, 20
Referring, 21
referring, 17, 21, 27
refers, 21
refilling, 66
reflects, 93
Regardless, 68, 76, 108
regardless, 101, 129
register, 128
regular, 17
relate, 94, 112
Related, 69, 77, 110
related, 55, 60, 71, 72, 75, 77, 78, 83, 84, 94, 131, 132, 133
relationship, 61, 64, 69, 70, 73, 108, 122
Release, 109
release, 109, 110, 116
relentlessly, 11

relevant, 132
Remember, 18, 127
remember, 127, 128
remembering, 127
renowned, 77
rent, 113, 134
Repair, 49
repeat, 63, 134
repeating, 58
repelling, 130
replaced, 10
Report, 47
report, 47, 48, 97, 98, 99
reports, 98
reputation, 80
request, 71, 90, 107
requesting, 43
require, 119, 134
required, 44, 62, 66, 108, 120
requires, 54, 72
reserved, 118
resistance, 119
rest, 54, 56, 73
restaurant, 25
result, 80, 116
Results, 125
results, 12, 25, 64, 72, 78, 90, 94, 108, 117, 125, 126
retaining, 118
retyping, 130
revenue, 104
review, 134

www.ingramcontent.com/pod-product-compliance
Lightning Source LLC
Chambersburg PA
CBHW051515170526
45165CB00002B/478